Set Your Heart Free

Francis de Sales

Foreword by Caroline Myss

Series Editor, John Kirvan

ave maria press AMP notre dame, indiana

Series Editor for 30 Days with a Great Spiritual Teacher: John Kirvan

Originally published as *Set Your Heart Free: The Practical Spirituality of Francis de Sales* in the 30 Days with a Great Spiritual Teacher series. For this work, early translations of various writings of Francis de Sales, primarily his letters and *An Introduction to the Devout Life,* have been distilled, freely adapted into modern English, combined, rearranged, and paraphrased into a format suitable for meditation. A translation published by Peter Reilly of Philadelphia has been especially helpful.

Not just this book, but this series owes an immeasurable debt to the Theological and College Libraries of St. John's Seminary in Camarillo, California, and to the unstinting courtesy and generosity of its librarians and staff, in a special way to Ron Hastings, Patricia Fessier, Sr. Francis Edward, and Lorraine de Necochea.

Founded in 1865, Ave Maria Press is a ministry of the United States Province of Holy Cross.

www.avemariapress.com

ISBN-10 1-59471-153-4   ISBN-13 978-1-59471-153-4

Cover and text design by Katherine Robinson Coleman.

Printed and bound in the United States of America.

Set Your Heart Free

So many in our culture are looking for "spiritual teachers" today. Mere repetition of formulas is no longer enough to feed our hungry souls. Here is solid, traditional, and yet revolutionary spiritual teaching from the ages! As with all great wisdom, you will find yourself saying, "I knew that . . . but I never heard it said so well, and I did not fully know it until this saint said it!"

Richard Rohr, O.F.M.
Center for Action and Contemplation, Albuquerque, New Mexico

These are glorious little books—concise and attractively designed! Distilled from the most influential writings in the Christian tradition, these pocket-sized books help you feel like you're having an intimate conversation with a wise counselor, a holy friend, or a beloved mentor. Give yourself a few minutes a day and let these holy men and women lead you to a closer relationship with the God who wants to be closer to you.

James Martin, S.J.
Author of *My Life with the Saints*

The 30 Days series shows how surprisingly similar the struggles and frustrations of these teachers are to our own daily challenges and distractions. Their wisdom also reminds us that daily challenges bring opportunities for grace and invite God to be part of our day. These spiritual teachers can help us to turn prayer into conversation with God, and the most mundane occasions become meetings with God in our neighbors.

Dr. Carolyn Y. Woo
Dean of Mendoza College of Business, University of Notre Dame

CONTENTS

FOREWORD

A mystical renaissance is at work in our world. Like a subtle field of grace that surrounds our world, individuals everywhere are exploring the seductive invitation to develop a joyful and intimate relationship with God. In keeping with the nature of this mystical awakening, more and more people are discovering the need to develop a more refined spiritual path. This new path that so many are drawn to today embodies characteristics once so familiar to the great mystics of the medieval and Renaissance eras. These mystics, our great spiritual teachers, include Teresa of Avila, Julian of Norwich, Francis of Assisi, St. John the Evangelist, Meister Eckhart, Francis de Sales, Catherine of Siena, Thérèse of Lisieux, Evelyn Underhill, and Mother Teresa in modern times.

Simply described, these mystics drew their strength from a devotion to prayer, contemplation, and self-reflection. They knew that a daily practice of time alone with God was required to review the day and reflect upon the well-being and harmony of their souls. Today, we are rediscovering the way in which they knew God. For all their differences, the common ground these mystics shared was a devotion to prayer and an unyielding faith in their mystical relationships with God.

As mystics in their day, these great spiritual teachers knew that God expected a great deal of them. God was, first of all, their most intimate companion. They knew the Divine through direct experience, not through intellectual discourse. Their lives were a continual Holy Communion with the Divine. That did not make their physical lives easy, and it didn't clear their paths of the boulders of fear and doubt. Such intimacy, however, did make their faith unrelenting and their understanding absolute in terms of what was real or unreal, authentic or illusory. They knew when God spoke directly to them and commanded them into action. "Francis," the Lord said, "rebuild my church." Perhaps Francis of Assisi paused for several moments, maybe even several days, wondering about that voice. But once he realized that God had spoken to him, he became illuminated with a fullness of grace. Nothing could dissuade him from his divine orders.

The mystics knew when to hold tight to their faith, especially when they were confronted with attacks from both inside and outside their monasteries. Attacks came mostly from those who envied the stamina in the souls of these saints. Mystical experiences and intimacy with the Divine do not translate into lives of ease. Rather, they produce people of truth, strength, and courage. No life path—even a mystic's—can alter the nature of life itself. Life is an ongoing journey of change and choice, a surrendering of the old and a trust in new beginnings. What these saints ultimately realized—and revealed to others—is that refining a relationship with God is the life choice on which all else is built.

Once that choice is made, it becomes your guide, no matter what difficulties life brings your way. No one can avoid hardships because life includes pain and heartache. But life can also include love and service to others and endless acts of creation on this earth. Love, service, and creation are legendary hallmarks in the lives of the saints. So, faith and prayer are not just resources we can turn to when we are in crisis. They are indispensable. As Teresa of Avila taught her nuns so well, "Learn to see God in the details of your life, for He is everywhere."

These wonderful mystics are enjoying a renewed popularity precisely because so many people are recognizing the need to find the Sacred once again. These men and women seek weekend retreats in monasteries just to be in the silence that was so familiar to those devoted full-time to contemplative life. The ordinary person, the "mystic out of a monastery," is now seeking an extraordinary spiritual life. If you are one of these, you will discover that the wisdom and the writings of these wondrous saints are as valuable today as they were hundreds of years ago. The truth is that the journey of the soul has never changed. We need to clearly mark that well-worn path to the Divine on which we see footprints of these saints.

In teaching about prayer, I am inevitably confronted with many questions from people. "What is prayer?" "How do I pray?" "What are the right prayers to say?" The awkwardness that people have around prayer reveals their awkwardness around God. We have built a culture on the intellectualizing of God. Talking about God or reading about what we think God is or is not can feel like a spiritual practice. But talking or reading about God is just that—no more and no less.

True prayer, on the other hand, is the practice of shutting down the mind and reflecting upon an elevated truth or mystical thought. This thought lifts you beyond the limitations of your five senses. In describing a mystical experience, Teresa wrote that her mind and eyes wanted to come with her, but they simply could not make the journey. Her senses were simply unable to withstand the presence of God. Only her soul had the stamina to be in the company of the Divine. In truth, these mystics realized what we all long to realize—intimacy with the Sacred. We are born with a yearning for God that we can try to fill with material goods and worldly accomplishments. At the end of the day, however, we are left wanting more. Julian of Norwich understood this so well, saying that ultimately, "Nothing less than God can satisfy us."

Life is an empty journey without the companionship of God. And developing a sense of divine intimacy requires time set aside to be with God in prayer, reflection, and contemplation. I am a passionate lover of Teresa of Avila, and I use her prayers daily. I find her prayer, "Let nothing disturb the silence of this moment with you, Oh Lord," the most comforting prayer I have ever found in my life. I repeat that praycr as often as a

dozen times a day. It brings me back into my castle,
back into my soul, and I am once again with God.
Immediately, I feel surrounded by a field of grace, no
matter where I am or what is happening around me.
Then I select some of her other prayers. With her
words, I close the drawbridge into my castle, withdraw-
ing from the world of my senses and from the clutter of
my mind. Alone with God, I dwell on Teresa's wisdom—
"If you have God you will want for nothing." Her words
lift me beyond the boundaries of my ordinary life. I
often feel as if I am hovering over my body, the tempo-
rary me experiencing—just for a second—the width and
breadth of eternity. Against that backdrop, I project
what is troubling me, and it vanishes. Such is the enduring power of prayer and grace in the pages of Teresa's
books.

The writings of Teresa and other mystics are alive
and full of grace in this series—30 Days with a Great
Spiritual Teacher. To read one of their prayers is to read
about their experiences of God. Take this grace into you
and let it take you away from the here and now of your
life. Let the wisdom of these teachers hover over your
life. Make contact with your own eternal self.

Caroline Myss
September 2007

Francis de Sales

For four-and-a-half centuries Francis de Sales has been in and out of style, at one moment riding the wave of popularity, at another left behind. Yet every generation that has read his books and letters has found in them a wise and warm, moderate and gentle companion for their spiritual journey. He comes across as psychologically insightful, as someone whose advice you can trust.

He was a nobleman, a scholar, a lawyer, a bishop, a religious founder, and, in time, a saint and a doctor of the Church. But nowhere in his writing does one get the feeling prevalent in so much classical spiritual literature that the author was reluctantly human. He was, as he told St. Jane de Chantal, "as human as anyone could possibly be."

But there was something else about his writing that was unique for his time and important to this day. Unlike so many others, he did not write for priests and nuns, for the walled spirituality of the cloister. He wrote for people with families to feed, clothe, and educate. While this is not uncommon today, what remains unusual is his ability to make the loftiest goals of mystical tradition accessible to men and women busy in the everyday workplace without compromising their demands.

Let Francis speak for himself:

> In the creation God commanded the plants of
> the earth to bring forth fruit, each after its kind; and
> in a similar way he commands Christians, who are
> the living plants of his church, to bring forth the
> fruits of devotion, each according to his calling and
> vocation. There is a different practice of devotion
> for the gentleman and the mechanic, for the prince
> and the servant, for the wife, the maiden and the
> widow. The practice of devotion must be adapted to
> the capabilities, the engagements, and the duties of
> each individual.

It would not do if the bishop were to adopt a
Carthusian solitude; if the father of a family refused,
like the Capuchins, to save money; if the artisan spent
his whole time in church like a professed religious; or if
the religious were to expose himself to all manners of
society on his neighbor's behalf as the bishop must do.
Such devotion would be inconsistent and ridiculous. Yet
this kind of mistake is not infrequently made, and the
world, being either not able or not willing to distinguish
between true devotion and the indiscretion of the false
devotee, condemns that devotion which nevertheless
has no share in these inconsistencies.

True devotion hinders no one, rather, it perfects
everything. Whenever it is out of keeping with any person's legitimate vocation, it must be spurious.

It is not merely an error but a heresy to suppose that
a devout life is necessarily banished from the soldier's

camp, the merchant's shop, the prince's court, or the domesticate's hearth.

In 1608, when first published, these words must have been somewhat shocking to a generation raised on the notion that high sanctity was very much the preserve of monks and nuns. Nearly four centuries later, it may not be shocking, but it is nevertheless reassuring to those with bills to pay *and* prayers to say.

It is also challenging.

HOW TO PRAY
THIS BOOK

The purpose of this book is to open a gate for you, to make accessible the spiritual insight and wisdom of one of history's most commonsense spiritual teachers, Francis de Sales.

Therefore it is not a book for mere reading. It invites you to meditate and pray its words on a daily basis over a period of thirty days and in a special way to enter into what Francis de Sales calls the "devout life."

It is a handbook for a special kind of spiritual journey.

Before you read the "rules" for taking this journey, remember that this book is meant to free your spirit, not confine it. If on any day the meditation does not resonate well for you, turn elsewhere to find a passage that seems to best fit the spirit of your day and your soul. Don't hesitate to repeat a day as often as you like until you feel that you have discovered what the Spirit, through the words of the author, has to say to your spirit.

To help you along the way, here are some suggestions for one way to use this book as a cornerstone of your daily prayers. They are based on the three forms of prayer central to Western spiritual tradition. The author of the classic *Cloud of Unknowing* has identified them as reading, reflection, and prayer. These three are so linked together that there can be no profitable reflection without first reading or hearing. Nor will beginners, or even the spiritually adept, come to true prayer

without first taking time to reflect on what they have
heard or read.

So for these thirty days there is a reading for the
start of each day developed from the writings of
Francis. There follows a meditation in the form of a
mantra to carry with you as a focus for the rest of your
day. And there is an exercise for bringing your day to an
end that asks you to find a place of quiet where you
might enter into silence and a final closure of your
reading and meditation. It is made up of, as Francis suggests, three classical prayer forms—thanksgiving, offering, and petition. We provide words of thanksgiving and
offering, but the prayer of petition is left up to your own
heart and imagination, your own feelings at the end of
another day.

These forms and suggestions, however, are not
meant to be constricting. Go where the Spirit leads you.

AS YOUR DAY BEGINS

As the day begins set aside a quiet moment in a
quiet place to do the reading provided for the day.

It is important to prepare to do the reading. Francis
is insistent that we begin by renewing our sense of
being in the presence of God.

We can recall that God is everywhere. "There is no
place in the world that he is not." We can recall even
more pointedly that "not only is God in this place where
you are, but that he is also in your own heart and spirit." A third method is to picture God looking down on

us. And a fourth is to picture the Lord by our side. He offers us choices and the good advice not to try them all at once. Do whatever is comfortable, but do something to place yourself consciously in God's presence as you begin your day. Whatever you do, he says, "make it short and simple."

This book begins the day with a reading from St. Francis de Sales. The passages are short. They never run more than a couple of hundred words, but they have been carefully selected to give a spiritual focus, a spiritual center to your whole day. They are designed to remind you as another day begins of your own existence at a spiritual level. They are meant to put you in the presence of the spiritual master who is your companion and teacher on this journey.

Do not be discouraged if you do not fully "get it" on your first reading. Don't be surprised if you understand nothing. In this thirty-day program you will be invited to do only what you can, to experience the Spirit in your own time and at your own pace. The effort required may prove to be exasperating, but it could also be an unusually rewarding spiritual experience.

A word of advice: proceed slowly. Very slowly. The passages have been broken down into sense lines to help you do just this. Don't read to get to the end, but to savor each word, each phrase, each image. There is no predicting, no determining in advance what short phrase, what word will trigger a response in your spirit. Give God a chance. After all, you are not reading these passages, you are praying them. You are establishing a mood of spiritual attentiveness for your whole day. What's the rush?

ALL THROUGH YOUR DAY

Immediately following the day's reading you will find a single sentence that Francis would call a nosegay, a gathering together of the heart of your reflections. It is a meditation in the form of a mantra, a word borrowed from the Hindu tradition. This phrase is meant to be a companion for your spirit as it moves through a busy day. Write it down on a 3" x 5" card or on the appropriate page of your daybook. Look at it as often as you can. Repeat it quietly to yourself, and go on your way.

It is not meant to stop you in your tracks or to distract you from responsibilities, but simply, gently, to remind you of the presence of God and your desire to respond to this presence.

You might consider carrying this mantric text from the day's reading with you in order to let its possible meaning for you sink more deeply into your imagination. Resist the urge to pull it apart, to make clean, clear, rational sense of it. A mantra is not an idea. It is a way of knowing God in a manner that emphasizes that the object of our search is immeasurably mysterious.

AS YOUR DAY IS ENDING

Francis is insistent that we end our daily meditation with three classical prayer forms. We have placed them at the end of the day. There is a prayer of thanksgiving, an offering, and a prayer of petition.

This is a time for letting go of the day, for entering a world of closing prayer.

For this period of prayer, we suggest that you choose a quiet, dark place that you can return to each day at its ending. When you come to it your first task is to quiet your spirit. Sit. You might be comfortable kneeling. Whatever stills your soul. Breath deeply. Inhale, exhale—slowly and deliberately, again and again until you feel your body let go of its tension.

Now, using the least possible light, follow the evening exercise slowly, phrase by phrase, stopping as your heart suggests. Use all three forms of prayer. Or use only one. Francis' advice is tested and true, but the Spirit moves where it wills.

If you find your mind arguing with the words, analyzing them, trying to figure out their meanings and goals, don't be surprised, but do start again by quieting your mind and freeing your imagination. Put behind you, as best you can, all that consciously or unconsciously stands between you and God.

All in all these prayers are an act of trust and confidence, an entry into peaceful sleep, a simple night prayer that gathers together the spiritual character of the day that is now ending as it began—in the presence of God. Look back with gratitude, forward with generosity, and above all in silent hope and confident prayer.

It is a time for summary and closure.

Invite God to embrace you with love and to protect you through the night.

Sleep well.

SOME OTHER WAYS TO USE THIS BOOK

1. Use it any way your spirit suggests. As mentioned earlier, skip a passage that doesn't resonate for you on a given day, or repeat for a second day or even several days a passage whose richness speaks to you. The truths of a spiritual life are not absorbed in a day, or, for that matter, in a lifetime. So take your time. Be patient with the Lord. Be patient with yourself.

2. Take two passages and/or their mantras—the more contrasting the better—and "bang" them together. Spend time discovering how their similarities or differences illumine your path.

3. Start a spiritual journal to record and deepen your experience of this thirty-day journey. Using either the mantra or another phrase from the reading that appeals to you, write a spiritual account of your day, a spiritual reflection. Create your own meditation.

4. Join millions who are seeking to deepen their spiritual life by joining with others to form a small group. More and more people are doing just this to support each other in their mutual quest. Meet once a week, or at least every other week, to discuss and pray about one of the meditations. There are many

books and guides available to help you make such a group effective.

John Kirvan, Series Editor

THIRTY DAYS WITH

FRANCIS DE SALES

DAY ONE

MY DAY BEGINS

An old proverb bids us
"make haste slowly."
Likewise King Solomon reminds us that
"hurried feet stumble."
And those who worry themselves sick
over every detail of their lives
do little,
and what little they do
they do poorly.
The noisiest bees
produce no honey.

We need to nourish our spirits
diligently and carefully,
but this is very different from
anxiety and debilitating worry.
Care and solicitude
don't undermine tranquility and peace of mind,
but anxiety and spiritual nitpicking,
to say nothing of upset and frenzy,
most certainly do.

13

Be conscientious
in all you are called upon to do,
but do not let
hurry, upset, anxiety, and nervousness,
get in the way
of common sense and good judgment,
and prevent you from doing well
what God calls you to do.

Our Lord rebuked Martha by calling her back
to the one thing necessary.

"Martha, Martha,
you are careful and troubled
about many things."

We may need to hear the same rebuke.

ALL THROUGH THE DAY

Be not troubled about many things.

MY DAY IS ENDING

With gratitude

Thank you for all the gifts of this day,
for making haste slowly

with my soul
lest I stumble.
For replacing my anxiety and preoccupation
with care and solicitude.
For reminding me
that only one thing is necessary:
trust in you.

With an offering

I offer you the silence of this night.
Let me not water it down
with a thousand distractions,
with the leftover cares of this day.

Let me give you instead a quiet mind,
a tranquil soul,
and a heart untroubled about many things.

And with a prayer for . . .

My Day Begins

Do not let anxiety
sabotage your search for God.

You know well
that when you search for something too anxiously
you can come upon it a hundred times
without ever seeing it.

Anxiety masquerades
as true spiritual energy,
even as it wearies our mind,
drains our enthusiasm,
and deadens our soul.

It pretends to stir up our souls,
but all it does is dampen our spirit.
It pushes us until
we stumble over our own feet.

We need to be on the watch for this impostor
that would have us believing
that our spiritual life
depends completely on our efforts,

so that the more panicked we are,
the more anxiously we search,
the more likely we are
to find God.

Let God do his part.
Be patient.

Not even our best efforts
can earn the blessings of God.

Our role is
to be ready,
to receive God's gifts
with an open heart—
carefully, humbly,
and serenely.

All Through the Day

Let God do his part.

My Day Is Ending

With gratitude

Thank you for all the gifts of this day.
In my impatience

to do it my way,
you alone know how many times today
I have stumbled over you
without ever recognizing you.

Thank you for your patience with me.

With an offering

I offer you the silence of this night.
Turn it into
a burning desire
that never mistakes nervous anxiety
for spiritual passion.

Take my silenced heart
and open it wide to your grace.
Do what only you can do
with what little I can offer you
from my poverty.

And with a prayer for . . .

DAY THREE

My Day Begins

Stop worrying.
Whatever it is that you must do
to follow the path
that God has shown you
do to the best of your ability.
And when you have done it,
move on to the next thing.

Don't keep rerunning it in your mind
trying to decide
whether your efforts were too little
or too much,
whether it was a great deed or a small one,
whether you might have done better.

If it wasn't sinful
and you were trying to do the will of God,
it is enough.

Don't worry. Move on.
Simply.
Calmly.

Peacefully.
Follow the path the Lord shows you
free of anxiety.
Otherwise
your anxiety will undermine
your efforts to grow.

If you do fail,
don't let anxiety
overcome you,
but admit your failure,
quietly, humbly,
and in God's presence.
Then get on with following the path
that God will continue to show you.

ALL THROUGH THE DAY

Don't worry!

MY DAY IS ENDING

With gratitude

Thank you for all the gifts of this day,
for blessing my efforts,
not caring

whether they were great or small,
done well or badly.

It mattered only
that I tried to do your will.
It was enough.
It always is.

With an offering

I offer you the silence of this night.
Take it,
and fill my soul
with the calm and peace
that comes from following
as best I can,
free of anxiety,
the path
you have laid out for me.

And with a prayer for . . .

DAY FOUR

....

MY DAY BEGINS

If you hope to succeed
in whatever you do,
place your trust totally in God's providence.
Cooperate with him,
then rest secure
that whatever happens,
will be best for you.

Think of a little child
walking with her father.
One hand clings tightly to his,
but with the other
she gathers fruit from trees along the way.

Imitate the child.
With one hand go ahead and gather
what you need of the world's good things,
but with the other
hold on to your heavenly Father,
checking regularly

whether or not
he approves of what you are doing with your life.

Above all,
beware of letting go of your Father
to free up both your hands
to gather more of the world's goods.
You will find
that by yourself
you will stumble and fall.

And when your gathering does not require
all your attention,
turn your mind to God as often as you can.
Like a sailor returning to port,
look to the sky
and not just to the waves that carry you.

ALL THROUGH THE DAY

Trust God, and rest secure.

MY DAY IS ENDING

With gratitude

Thank you for all the gifts of this day,
especially for taking me by the hand.

Thank you too,
for all the good things of this world
that you have this day put within my reach.

In you I trust.
In you is my security.

With an offering

I offer you the silence of this night,
these closing moments of my day
when my gathering can be put aside.
Let me turn my mind to you.
Here in the dark
I am the sailor returning to port,
looking to the sky
and not just to the waves
that carry me through the day.

And with a prayer for . . .

DAY FIVE

....

MY DAY BEGINS

Don't waste your time
dreaming of being someone else.
Don't try to be someone else.
Work and pray
at being yourself.

Be who you are,
where you are.
Concentrate
on the little everyday problems and pains
that beset you.

Reserve your best efforts,
expend your spiritual energy
on what is right before you.
This is what God asks of you.

This is all he asks of you:
that you live
and respond to his grace
in the here and now.
To do anything else is to waste your time.

Listen closely.
This is very important—
and very misunderstood—
for we all prefer to do
what is to our personal liking.
Very few of us choose duty first,
or the will of God.

Don't cultivate someone else's garden.
Grow where you are planted.

ALL THROUGH THE DAY

Be who you are.

MY DAY IS ENDING

With gratitude

Thank you for all the gifts of this day,
especially for loving
and gracing
the person I am.

Thank you for the garden
in which you have placed me
and where alone I will find you.

With an offering

I offer you the silence of this night.
Take what you ask of me,
and what I alone can offer you:
a life lived
responding to your grace
in the here and now,
in the only world I have,
the world that lies right before me.

This is all you ask of me:
This is all I have to give.

And with a prayer for . . .

DAY SIX

....

MY DAY BEGINS

Many of us make the mistake
of building our spiritual lives
around major crises and great opportunities.
We leave ourselves
totally unprepared
to deal with and take advantage of
the little ones
that are presented to us
day in and day out.

It would actually be better
to concentrate less on the great but rare events
and to be ready for and open to
the constant little ones
that are the stuff of everyday living.

We are all
obliged to strive for perfection,
as both Christ and St. Paul tell us.
But we need to remember
that perfection consists

of doing the will of God,
of using that will
as the standard for all our decisions,
great and small.

We are to flee what God wants us to avoid
and bring about
what he wants us to achieve in his name.
And we are to do this
not only in large matters
and serious trials,
but even in minor upsets
and little opportunities.

It is one thing, and rather dramatic,
to prepare for a happy death,
but it is just as important
to be ready, with undramatic patience,
to face each new day and its trivial trials.

All Through the Day

Patience—day in, day out.

MY DAY IS ENDING

With gratitude

Thank you for all the gifts of this day,
for a day filled
with a thousand trivial trials
and little opportunities,
and for the strength
I borrowed from you
in those scattered moments when
I recognized your presence
and responded to it as best I could.

With an offering

I offer you the silence of this night.
Accept my little responses
to the little things
that make up my life.

Take the little deaths
that I must die,
from moment to moment,
and weave of them
a death to all but you.

And with a prayer for . . .

DAY SEVEN

....

MY DAY BEGINS

The way to honor God,
whose handiwork we are,
is to be who we are,
as perfectly as we can.

It is enough to be
what God wants us to be,
rather than some perfect creature
that God never had in mind.

Suppose you were
the most perfect being
you could possibly imagine.
So what?
If you were not the person
God had in mind
at the moment of your creation,
what good would it do you?

It is also enough
to do whatever it is
that you can do

being who you are, and where you are.
Just do wholeheartedly
what you know God is asking of you.
Don't bother yourself
about whether or not
what God asks of you is important and grand.
Whether your actions are
insignificant or not
does not matter,
if they are God's will.

How could you be disappointed
at even the smallest opportunity
if you know that it is God's will—
born of his providential concern for you,
and chosen for you
in his eternal wisdom?

ALL THROUGH THE DAY

Be who you are.

MY DAY IS ENDING

With gratitude

Thank you for all the gifts of this day,
for letting me understand,

as this day ends,
that even the smallest opportunity
that comes my way
carries with it your eternal wisdom.
Your will for me,
is the seed
of all you want for me.

With an offering

I offer you the silence of this night.
Accept as a measure
of my hope
whatever it is
that I can do,
being who I am,
where I am.
You will not, I know,
be disappointed.
Help me not to be.

And with a prayer for . . .

DAY EIGHT

••

My Day Begins

Don't think
that you can overcome in a day
the bad habits of a lifetime,
or enjoy perfect spiritual health
after years of inattention.

Be patient.

As long as we live
we will bear the burden of ourselves,
the limitations of our humanity.
Perfection will have to wait
for another life,
another world.

Of course,
God has cured some people instantly,
leaving no trace of their former failures.
Think of Mary Magdalene.
In an instant
Jesus brought her from a life of sin
to a life of holiness.

But that same God
left many of his most loyal disciples
weakened by their past.
Think of Peter
who fell often.
On one occasion
he went so far as to deny the Lord.

God will do what is best for us.

Most likely
he will lead us little by little,
one small step at a time,
So we need to be patient with everyone,
with everything,
but especially with ourselves
and with God.

ALL THROUGH THE DAY

Perfection may have to wait.

MY DAY IS ENDING

With gratitude

Thank you for all the gifts of this day,
for doing

what is best for me,
for leading me little by little,
one small step at a time.
Thank you for helping me carry
the burden of myself,
the limitations of my own humanity.

With an offering

I offer you the silence of this night.
I cannot offer you perfection,
only a soul weak with
the bad habits of a lifetime
and years of inattention.
But what I have
I offer you,
knowing, as you have taught me,
that perfection will have to wait.

And with a prayer for . . .

DAY NINE

MY DAY BEGINS

The biggest mistake
that most of us make about God,
the one that most consistently
undermines our peace of soul,
is the idea
that God demands a lot of us,
more than fragile beings like ourselves,
could ever give.

Such a God is frightening.

But God in reality is content
with the little we can give,
because God knows—
and accepts—
the little that we have.

We need to do just three things:

Do the best we can
to find and honor God
in everything we do.

Do whatever—however little—
we can to live this way.

Let God do the rest.

If we follow these simple rules,
we will possess God.
And possessing God
we will not be disturbed,
we will not be anxious,
for we will have no need
to fear a God,
who never asks of us
more than we can give.

ALL THROUGH THE DAY

God is content with the little we have.

MY DAY IS ENDING

With gratitude

Thank you for all the gifts of this day,
for asking of me only what I could give,
even when it seemed to me
to be so little,
and so unworthy of you.

Thank you
for not making me
afraid to offer you so little.

With an offering

I offer you the silence of this night.
Out of empty pockets and empty hands,
I offer you the riches
of a soul struggling
to do the best I can
to honor you
in every way I can
with the little that I have.
I leave the rest to you.

And with a prayer for . . .

DAY TEN

MY DAY BEGINS

The more we recall and appreciate
the mercies of God—
especially those private, secret mercies
that no one else is aware of—
the more we shall love him.

But it is a humbling experience.
Face to face
with the compassion of God
we see the abundance of his mercies.
But in the same moment
we are faced with his justice
and must acknowledge
the abundance of our misdeeds.

Let us reflect, therefore,
upon all he has done for us,
and acknowledge his mercies
even as we number our sins.
It will not be an occasion for pride.

Even a mule laden with precious jewels
is still a mule.

Paul says, "What do you have
that you have not received?
And since you have received it
why do you act
as though you have not received it?"
Should we be tempted to take credit
for what virtues we have,
we need only remember
our ingratitude,
our imperfections,
our weakness.

What have you managed to do without God?

It is all right to rejoice in our deeds,
and rejoice in having done them,
just so long as we give all the ensuing glory to God,
who is their author.

All Through the Day

What do I have
that I have not received?

MY DAY IS ENDING

With gratitude

Thank you for all the gifts of this day.
Even though I have nothing
that I have not received from you,
more often than not, I must admit,
I act as though
I do everything on my own.
But even if it is just for this quiet moment,
let me acknowledge my debt,
and from my heart,
thank you.

With an offering

I offer you the silence of this night.
Everything I have,
including this quiet moment,
is your gift to me.
Let me surrender my hold on it
so that you might use it
as you wish
and so that I might find your mercy there.

And with a prayer for . . .

DAY ELEVEN

MY DAY BEGINS

Humility is as humility does!

Sometimes we confess that we are nothing,
that we are weakness itself,
the very dust of the earth.
But we get very upset
if someone takes us at our word.

We conspicuously retreat into solitude
and hide ourselves,
but with the hope
that the world will "discover" us.

We take the lowest place,
cherishing the hope
that we will be asked to go up higher.

True humility does not go about
looking and sounding humble.
For the humble person prefers
to hide her virtues,
and conceal her true self,
to live unknown, in a concealed life.

My advice then is that you should
go easy with your expressions of humility,
making sure that your deep inward feelings
agree with whatever you say outwardly.

Never cast down your eyes
without humbling your heart,
and do not pretend
that you wish to be among the least
unless you truly desire it in your heart.

Really humble people
would rather have others say that
they are contemptible and worth nothing,
than say it about themselves.

ALL THROUGH THE DAY

Walk humbly in the truth.

MY DAY IS ENDING

With gratitude

Thank you for all the gifts of this day.
They are not for display,
for public parading,
or for posturing,
but for silent gratitude.

Here in your presence
let me say
only what I know to be true.

With an offering

I offer you the silence of this night.

Here in its darkness and solitude
I admit that I am nothing,
that I am the dust of the earth.

You can take me at my word.
At least here.
At least now.

And with a prayer for . . .

DAY TWELVE

MY DAY BEGINS

A heart that is free
is the close companion
of a peaceful soul.

A free heart is one
that is not attached to its own way
of doing things,
that does not become impatient
when things don't go its way.
A free heart
will surely enjoy spiritual consolations,
but is not dependent on them
and will, to the best of its ability,
accept troubles in their stead.

A free heart
is not so tied
to a schedule or a way of praying
that any change is upsetting
and a source of anxiety.
A free heart

is not attached
to what is beyond its control.

A free heart prays to God
that his name be hallowed,
that his kingdom come,
that his will be done,
on earth as it is in heaven.

For if the name of God is hallowed,
if his kingdom is in us,
if his will is being done,
a free spirit need not concern itself
with anything else.

ALL THROUGH THE DAY

Set my heart free.

MY DAY IS ENDING

With gratitude

Thank you for all the gifts of this day,
for the moments of freedom
when your will
was done,
when your kingdom grew within me,

and my heart
concerned itself
with nothing else.

With an offering

I offer you the silence of this night,
that you might make my heart
free of attachments
to my own way of doing things.

And I offer you my soul
that you might bring it peace,
and when things don't go my way,
patience.

And with a prayer for . . .

DAY THIRTEEN

....

MY DAY BEGINS

Do you remember how,
when you were a small child,
you would take an abandoned carton
or a fistful of sand
and turn it into a castle?

Inevitably, it seemed,
someone would knock it over.
Your heart would be broken.

But now we understand that those things
that were so earthshaking
when we were children
were in the end not all that important.
Our world did not end when our castles fell.

Yet here we are,
still frantic and anxious
about the frail castles of our adult years.
They too will fall
and it will not matter that much
in the light of eternity.

But it takes a while
to gain this perspective.

We can spend our days
running in circles,
obsessed by a thousand things,
convinced that each one of them
is all-important to our happiness.

Or we can stop for a moment
and think of eternity.
Then we see how very unimportant
are the thousand concerns
that clutter our minds
and preoccupy our souls.

How little they matter!

ALL THROUGH THE DAY

What really matters?

MY DAY IS ENDING

With gratitude

Thank you for all the gifts of this day,
for letting me end this day
remembering

that however frantic and anxious
I might have been
about the frail castles of my life,
in the light of eternity,
they do not matter.

With an offering

I offer you the silence of this night.
Take the abandoned cartons
and bits of sand
out of which
I still build my castles
and make of these frail dreams,
these scattered, hurried moments
of my day,
something that will last
through eternity.

And with a prayer for . . .

DAY FOURTEEN

....

My Day Begins

"Learn from me," Jesus said,
"for I am meek and humble of heart."

"Learn from me," he was saying,
"to be patient and gentle
with your neighbor,
and humble before my Father."

"Learn from me," he was saying,
"to be patient and gentle with everyone,
but especially with yourself."

Don't be anxious
to condemn yourself
every time you fall.
Instead, patiently, gently,
pick yourself up
and start all over again.

There is no better way
to grow toward perfection
than to be willing—

and patient enough—
to start over again and again.

To follow this simple advice
is to discover the secret
of a truly devout life.

God will give you
an inward peace
and all the patience you need,
but you must sincerely ask him for it.
And you must put it to work, day by day.
Use every opportunity
to perform acts of patient gentleness,
no matter how small they may seem at the time,
for our Lord has promised:
"To the person who is faithful in little things,
greater ones will be given."

All Through the Day

"Learn from me!"

My Day Is Ending

With gratitude

Thank you for all the gifts of this day,

for teaching me,
by your own example,
that patience is the way to perfection.
Let me learn from you
to be patient with everyone,
but especially
with myself.

With an offering

I offer you the silence of this night.
Accept the offerings of my impatient soul
and fill it with your peace.

Use the hours of this night
to plant in my soul
the seeds of a patience
that will enclose everyone around me,
but especially
myself.

And with a prayer for . . .

DAY FIFTEEN

....

MY DAY BEGINS

When you are in love,
lovers say,
the whole world
speaks of the one you love

It is hard to think of anything else.
Your heart overflows.
When you speak,
it is hard not to speak of him.
And when you are silent,
you daydream about her.
This absence of your beloved is intolerable.

So, too,
those who love God
are never weary of thinking of him,
living for him,
yearning for him,
and talking of him.
To them,
the whole world

speaks in a silent language of love,
exciting them
to thoughts of the one they love—
exciting us, if we listen
to thoughts of the one we love—
firing an insatiable yearning
to be in his presence.

Speak, then,
when you are spoken to.
Do not be embarrassed
to acknowledge
that everywhere and always
you hear
the voice of the one you love.
Go where
your heart takes you.

All Through the Day

Speak when you are spoken to.

My Day Is Ending

With gratitude

Thank you for all the gifts of this day,
especially for never staying
far from my thoughts,
for being everywhere I looked,
for filling every silence with your voice,
for giving me a reason
to speak with you
at every turn.

With an offering

I offer you the silence of this night
to fill with your voice.

I offer you this darkness
to fill with your light.

I offer you this solitude
to fill with your presence.

I offer you what I have
and who I am.

And with a prayer for . . .

DAY SIXTEEN

MY DAY BEGINS

With persistent caring
our heavenly Father
is forever planting in our hearts
gentle inspirations that he hopes
will awaken and kindle in us
a desire for his heavenly love.

Receive them
gratefully, reverently, and without hesitation.
Listen to them meekly.
Cultivate the love you feel.

Finding joy in these inspirations
may not seem like much,
but it is a great step.
For even though such delight
falls far short of complete commitment to his love,
it still demonstrates
that we are moving,
however slowly, however cautiously,
in the right direction.

Do not forget, however,
that perfection lies in acting on these inspirations,
for if, after welcoming them gladly,
we fail to act on them,
we greatly offend God
and trivialize his goodness.

Do not stop, therefore,
with his inspirations,
but follow through on them
fully, lovingly, and ceaselessly.
For then our Father
who is under no obligation to us,
may hold himself obliged by our love.

A consent that remains nestled in the heart
and produces no outward results
is like a vine that bears no fruit.

All Through the Day

Perfection is in acting
on our Father's inspirations.

MY DAY IS ENDING

With gratitude

Thank you for all the gifts of this day,
for planting
in all its corners
tiny reminders of your presence,
gentle inspirations
meant to blossom into love.

Please don't stop now!
Cultivate them in me
in all the days to come.

With an offering

I offer you in the silence of this night
the fragile fruit
planted this day.

It is not meant
to remain a warm seed
protected in my heart.
Let it grow.
Let me share it with whomever I meet
when tomorrow comes.

And with a prayer for . . .

DAY SEVENTEEN

MY DAY BEGINS

It is through patience,
as the Lord himself reminds us,
that we achieve great happiness,
that we come to possess our soul.

The more perfect our patience is,
the more perfect our happiness.

We need, therefore, to remind ourselves frequently
that it was by patient suffering
that our Lord saved us.

We can expect
to work out our salvation
in the same way,
enduring our injuries, contradictions, and annoyances
with his great calm and gentleness—
with his patience—
embracing every sort of trial
that he sends us
or permits to overtake us.

Some people are willing, of course,
to suffer things that bring honor with them,
(to be wounded in war or taken prisoner, for example,
or to be ill-treated because of their religion),
but they can be more in love
with the honor
than patient with the suffering.

The truly patient servant of God
does not pick and choose,
but bears in patience
whatever comes her way,
the reproach of the good
as well as the contempt of the wicked,
the honorable
and the merely annoying.

ALL THROUGH THE DAY

It is in patience
that we shall possess our souls.

MY DAY IS ENDING

With gratitude

Thank you for all the gifts of this day,

for all the things
that came my way,
from the truly troubling
to the merely annoying,
and for the grace
to demonstrate
from time to time
the little patience that I have.

With an offering

I offer you the silence of this night,
wrapped now
in patience.
I make a gift of the injuries,
the contradictions, and annoyances
not just of this day,
but all those I have
saved up
and fed over a lifetime.

And with a prayer for . . .

DAY EIGHTEEN

....

MY DAY BEGINS

True patience accepts,
not only the great and heavy trials
that occasionally come our way,
but also the petty troubles
and annoying accidents of everyday.

This means being patient
not only in the face of great sickness,
but with minor annoyances,
that God sends or permits.
It means being patient
with where he wills us to be,
patient with those
with whom he has surrounded us,
patient with whatever circumstances he permits.

Do not, however,
confuse patience
with indifference, laziness,
or lack of common sense.

When you are overtaken by misfortune,
seek whatever remedies God affords you.
Not to do so
would be tempting his divine providence.

When, however,
you have done whatever you can do,
used whatever God has put within your reach,
await the outcome
with patient resignation.
If God sees fit
to overcome the evils,
cure the illness, or whatever,
thank him humbly.
But if, on the other hand,
he permits the evil to triumph,
patiently bless his holy name
and surrender yourself
to his will for you.

All Through the Day

Patience is not laziness.

MY DAY IS ENDING

With gratitude

Thank you for all the gifts of this day,
for the place I spent it
and for those with whom I spent it,
for all its joys
and all its sorrows,
for the troubles overcome
and for those that remain.

With an offering

I offer you the silence of this night,
its darkness and its solitude.
Whether you choose
under the cover of this night
to take away the problems of this day,
or leave them for tomorrow,
I will bless your name.

Thy will be done.

And with a prayer for . . .

DAY NINETEEN

My Day Begins

The person who dives for pearls
is never satisfied to come up with shells.
Neither should those who aim at virtue
be satisfied
with honors and reputation.

The more virtue parades itself,
the more it desires to be seen and acclaimed,
the less likely it is
to be real and true.

True virtue and personal attractiveness
are not rooted and supported
in pride, self-sufficiency, and vanity.
These produce a life lived
strictly for show.
It blooms brilliantly
and quickly withers away.

Having the appearance of virtue
may be fine for those
who do not seek it,

who accept it indifferently,
and who do not mistake the shell for the pearl.
But it can become very dangerous and hurtful
to those who cling to it,
and take delight in it.

For if someone
is truly wise, truly learned,
truly generous and noble,
this person's gifts will flower
in true humility and modesty.

A really great soul
will not waste himself on such empty goods
as rank, honor, and form.
This person has higher aspirations.

ALL THROUGH THE DAY

Seek the pearl, not the shell.

MY DAY IS ENDING

With gratitude

Thank you for all the gifts of this day,
and especially
for reminding me

that quiet humility and modesty,
not self-sufficiency and vanity,
are the ground in which
I must plant my hopes
if my soul is to grow
and not wither.

With an offering

I offer you the silence of this night,
and whatever honor or recognition
might have come to me today.
I return it to you
its source,
its life,
its flower.

And with a prayer for . . .

MY DAY BEGINS

We do what we can
to find the peace of Christ,
and he does the rest.
But this does not mean
that there is no price to be paid.
Almost certainly
we will need
to leave behind
much that we have clung to,
the familiarity and comfort
of being self-sufficient,
our reassuring self-confidence,
our abounding self-love.

It will be painful.
As the scriptures say,
to separate us from our self-love,
he will bring
"not peace but the sword."
His sword will leave our hearts raw.

We will resist, with our whole beings,
the wrenching that precedes peace.
It's true, however,
that, in the end,
if we remain committed to finding
the will of God,
and do our own small bit,
faithfully and courageously,
he will do the rest.
His promised peace will come.

"Let not my will, but yours be done."

Our peace will be found
in the midst of warfare;
our serenity will be bought
at the price of surrender.

All Through the Day

Do what you can,
God will do the rest.

My Day Is Ending

With gratitude

Thank you for all the gifts of this day,

for making it easier,
as the day ends
and I slip into silent darkness,
to cut myself free from
my self-love,
to gratefully accept
"not peace but the sword."

I thank you.

With an offering

I offer you the silence of this night
and a heart
ready to surrender,
a will ready to bend
to your desires for me.

"Let not my will, but yours be done."
Let your promised peace be mine
even at the cost of a war within my heart.

And with a prayer for . . .

DAY TWENTY-ONE

MY DAY BEGINS

Because we become what we love,
we will ourselves become truly poor
only by loving poverty and the poor.

"Who is weak and I am not weak?"
says St. Paul.
He might have continued:
"Who is poor and I am not poor?"
Love makes us like those we love.
If then we truly love the poor,
truly enter into their poverty,
we will be poor with them.

We cannot love the poor
by keeping at a distance,
but only by being with them,
by visiting them,
by talking freely, openly with them,
by being with them
in the church, on the street,

wherever poverty leads,
wherever need is present.
Speak with everyone
out of your own poverty,
but let your hands be rich,
sharing freely of what you have.

Blessed are they who are poor,
for theirs truly is the kingdom of heaven.
To them, the King of Kings
who is King of the Poor
will say on the day of judgment:
"I was hungry
and you gave me to eat,
I was naked,
and you covered me.
Come
possess the kingdom prepared for you
from the beginning of the world."

ALL THROUGH THE DAY

Who is poor and I am not poor?

My Day Is Ending

With gratitude

Thank you for all the gifts of this day.
I was hungry
and you gave me to eat.
I was naked
and you covered me.
I was homeless
and you called me
to possess the kingdom prepared for me
and for all the poor, naked, and homeless.

With an offering

I offer you the silence of this night,
and the poverty of my soul.
Love makes us like those we love,
and you have loved me.
You have not kept your distance.
You have entered into my poverty.
You have greeted me with a full hand.
You have gone where poverty drew you.
Let me follow in your steps.

And with a prayer for . . .

My Day Begins

A good name is like a sign
pointing to a virtuous life,
and though it is a good sign
it is still just a sign.
To be overly sensitive about it
is to become like a hypochondriac
who busies himself
taking medicine for every passing symptom.
He intends to preserve his health
but ends up ruining it.

If you try to stay in everyone's good graces
you can end up being friends with no one.
On the other hand, you may be overly sensitive.
And after all, who wants to be around
people whose touchiness makes them unbearable?

But what underlies such spiritual hypochondria
is what matters most.

Fear for your good name
can mean that

you are not putting your trust
in its only true foundation—
the solid stone of real virtue.

If, because of your spiritual efforts,
someone calls you a hypocrite, pay her no heed.
If you are quick to forgive an injury, and
someone else calls you a coward,
ignore him.

His judgments matter not at all.
He may damage your name
but his foolish chatter,
his shallow judgments,
cannot destroy what is true.

All Through the Day

Trust who you are,
not what "they" think you are.

My Day Is Ending

With gratitude

Thank you for all the gifts of this day,
but especially for being the stone

on which I can build
the good life I seek.

Your opinion alone matters.

It is in your good graces alone
that I desire to be.

With an offering

I offer you the silence of this night
in which the silly chatter
and the shallow judgments of others
are stilled for the moment
and I can turn to you
in confidence
and trust.
Be my foundation,
now and forever.

And with a prayer for . . .

DAY TWENTY-THREE

My Day Begins

We are on a journey to a more blessed life.
Let us not, along the way
be angry with one another.
Instead let us go forward with our fellow travelers,
our brothers and sisters,
gently, in peace and in love.
And whatever happens along the way,
however great the provocation,
do not let anger into your heart.
Take with you the advice of Joseph
when he bid his brothers good-bye:
"Be not angry along the way."

Don't let anger get the smallest foothold
in your heart.
Exclude absolutely, as Augustine advises,
even its slightest presence,
however justified and reasonable
it may seem.
For once it gets into your heart
it is hard to uproot.

A mote rapidly becomes a beam.
It will stay with you
and if you ignore the apostle Paul's advice,
and let the sun go down on your anger,
it will harden into hatred.
Constantly fed by
imaginings and delusions,
it will become all but impossible
to set yourself free of it.

It is best to avoid all anger
rather than try to come to terms with it;
for if we give anger an inch
it will surely take a mile.

ALL THROUGH THE DAY

Be not angry along the way.

MY DAY IS ENDING

With gratitude

Thank you for all the gifts of this day,
for my fellow travelers,
my brothers and sisters

who in peace and love
are your special gifts to me.

With an offering

I offer you the silence of this night
where there is no place for anger.
Let the sun go down gently
on a heart warmed by peace and love
for my fellow travelers
on the way
to a blessed life with you.

And with a prayer for . . .

DAY TWENTY-FOUR

....

MY DAY BEGINS

Whenever your spirit is troubled,
take some advice from St. Augustine:

"Make haste, like David, to cry out:
'Have mercy on me, O Lord,'
that he may stretch forth his hand
to moderate your anger
or whatever it is that troubles you."

Imitate the apostles
who when they found themselves
caught in a raging storm,
called upon God to help them.
He will still your anger
as he stilled the seas
and replace it with his peace.

Remember however, to pray calmly and gently.

As soon as you are aware
of having given into anger or whatever,
repair your mistake immediately
with an act of kindness
to the person you have hurt.

If you tell a lie,
the best thing
is to recall it
as soon as you can.

The best cure for anger
is an immediate act of gentleness.

New wounds are the easiest to heal.

ALL THROUGH THE DAY

Have mercy on me, O Lord.

MY DAY IS ENDING

With gratitude

Thank you for all the gifts of this day,
for responding to my anger
with your gentleness,
for answering my petty lies
with your truth,
for healing my wounds
and those I have wounded.

With an offering

I offer you the silence of this night

and a soul too often troubled.
Have mercy on me, O Lord.
Stretch forth your hand.
Rescue me from the storms
that threaten my soul,
and replace them
with your peace.

And with a prayer for . . .

MY DAY BEGINS

It doesn't take much
to remind us of our fragility.

At any moment,
however lofty our prayers,
however convinced we are of our spiritual strength,
we can find ourselves
with little or no notice,
plunged into chilling reality,
humbly pleading for God to save us.

Think of Peter.
There he was,
so sure of his faith,
that he stepped from the boat
to walk on water.
But when the wind came up unexpectedly
and the waves became threatening,
he was quick to cry out:
"Lord, save me!"
The response of Jesus was just as swift.

He reached out and took Peter by the hand,
but then he chided him:
"Where is your faith?
Why do you doubt?"

Is it any different with us?
Doesn't it often take
the winds of temptation,
our overconfident steps,
to bring us to call upon God?

We lose our footing
and God takes us by the hand.
"Where is your faith?" he asks.
"Why do you doubt?"

Where indeed?
Why indeed?

ALL THROUGH THE DAY

Where is my faith?

MY DAY IS ENDING

With gratitude

Thank you for all the gifts of this day,

for taking me by the hand
whenever my faith deserted me
and I lost my footing,
whenever I forgot
that you alone can hold me up.

Thank you for being there
whenever I doubt.

With an offering

I offer you the silence of this night.
Take the foolhardy and brave gestures
that I make to impress you,
and see in them a heart
that yearns to truly love you.
For to believe in you
is to walk on water.
Knowing that you will hold me up,
knowing too that when my heart falters
you will still be there
to take me by the hand.

And with a prayer for . . .

MY DAY BEGINS

When it comes to being gentle,
start with yourself.

Don't get upset
with your imperfections.
Being disappointed by failure
is understandable,
but it shouldn't turn into
bitterness or spite directed at yourself.

It's a great mistake—
because it leads nowhere—
to get angry because you are angry,
upset at being upset,
disappointed because you are disappointed.

So don't fool yourself.
You cannot correct a mistake
by repeating it.
Anger is no remedy for anger.
It's just a seed-bed
for renewed anger.

And don't fool yourself into thinking
that self-recrimination is a sign of virtue.
It is a sign of self-love.
You are not perfect.

Try then to take your failings in stride.
Look at yourself calmly, gently,
with clear-thinking regret.
Quiet, steady repentance
is far more effective
than emotional upset.
It goes far deeper
and lasts far longer.

ALL THROUGH THE DAY

Anger is not the remedy for anger.

MY DAY IS ENDING

With gratitude

Thank you for all the gifts of this day,
for the gifts of your gentleness,
your patience,
and above all,

your lack of anger
with my anger,
your lack of disappointment
with my disappointment.

With an offering

I offer you the silence of this night,
all the disappointments,
all the seeds of anger
that I planted this day,
that I carry to the edge
of its silence and solitude.
Lift them from my soul
and replace them with your peace.

And with a prayer for . . .

DAY TWENTY-SEVEN

....

My Day Begins

Why are you surprised
when the weak turn out to be weak,
and the frail, frail?
When you turn out to be sinful?

When you fall
be gentle with your frail, weak heart.

Lift up your heart gently,
accept your failure
without wallowing in your weakness.
Admit your guilt in God's sight.
Then with good heart,
with courage and confidence in his mercy,
start over again.

It is tempting to condemn yourself
with harsh words
and even harsher feelings.
But it does no good
to lash out at yourself.

Seek instead to rebuild your soul
calmly, reasonably, and compassionately.

Speak to your heart in understanding words:

"Rise up my heart still another time.
Put your trust in God's mercy,
so that you will stand stronger in the future.
Do not be discouraged,
God will help and guide you."

Pray with the Psalmist:
"Why are you sad my soul,
and why do you disquiet me?
Hope in God:
for I will still give praise to him;
the salvation of my countenance,
and my God."

ALL THROUGH THE DAY

Lift up your heart—but gently!

MY DAY IS ENDING

With gratitude

Thank you for all the gifts of this day,

for lifting up my heart gently
when I fell.
For the gift of courage and confidence
in your mercy,
that left me able
to start over again.

With an offering

I offer you the silence of this night.
Let there be no room in it for sadness.
This is not the time for disquiet.
It is a time for hope and praise,
a time for salvation.
So do not be sad my soul.
Praise God
in the dark and solitude
he has given you.

And with a prayer for . . .

MY DAY BEGINS

God welcomes us into his presence
always and everywhere.
We need not wait
until our heart is overflowing with words,
or our soul burdened with needs
before we present ourselves.

It is enough to be there.
It is all right to be speechless.
After all,
the primary reason for entering God's presence
is simply to acknowledge him
and to offer him
the honor that is his due.

We don't need words for this.
We need only to be there,
to let our presence speak
what is deepest in our soul.
He is our God,
we are his creatures.

Our soul bows down before him
in honor and praise
awaiting his will for us.
Think of how
politicians and others
go into the presence of their leaders
over and over again,
not to speak to them
or to hear them speak
but just to be seen!

But we are not mere time-servers,
fawning followers.
We are seekers after God,
and we come before him
to demonstrate
our love and fidelity,
our wordless joy
merely at being in his presence.

ALL THROUGH THE DAY

We need only be there.

MY DAY IS ENDING

With gratitude

Thank you for all the gifts of this day,
for letting me
into your presence,
speechless though I was.

And thank you
for accepting
my wordless joy
merely at being in your presence.

With an offering

I offer you the silence of this night.
I have no great words
to offer you.
Here in the gathering darkness
I am still speechless.
So take my silent presence,
awake or asleep,
and make of it
a prayer
that says
what I have no words to express.

And with a prayer for . . .

MY DAY BEGINS

Sometimes, of course,
when we enter into God's presence
we will not find ourselves speechless.

We will be ready
to speak to him
and to hear what he has to say to us.

Usually he will respond
in quiet inspirations
and in the silent movement
of our heart.

His voice will fill our souls
with consolation and courage.

So if you are able to speak to the Lord,
do it with words of prayer.

Praise him.
Listen to him.

But if, no matter how full your heart is
with things you wish to say to God,

your voice still fails you,
stay right where you are
in his presence.
He will see you there,
and bless your silence.
And perhaps he will reach down
and take you by the hand,
walking with you,
chatting with you,
leading you gently
through the garden
of his love.

Whatever happens,
it is a great grace.

All Through the Day

Speak to him. Listen to him.

My Day Is Ending

With gratitude

I thank you for all the gifts of this day,
for all the moments of this day
when you took me by the hand,

walked with me,
chatted with me,
and led me gently
through the garden
of your love.

With an offering

I offer you the silence of this night.
Take what words I have,
what little courage
my heart can muster,
and build on them.
Above all accept and bless
my willingness to hear you
when you speak
with quiet inspiration
into the silence
of this night.

And with a prayer for . . .

DAY THIRTY

My Day Begins

There are three things about living in peace
that you should never forget.

Peace does not mean
living without pain.
You lose peace
not when you are trouble free,
but when you cease
to be dependent on God
and fail in your duties.

You must expect pain
and not be disturbed by it.
Our set ways of doing things
are not let go of easily.
They give way to the "new person" in God
with great reluctance.
Don't be disturbed.
You have not lost favor with God.
God is never
the source of our anxiety.

Because anxiety is the enemy of peace,
it cannot come from God.
It is an enemy of the spirit.
Treat anxiety like the temptation it is.
Fight it.
Send it on its way.

Whatever you must do,
whether it is
defending yourself against temptation
or welcoming joy,
do it peacefully,
without anxiety.

You cannot keep your peace by losing it.

ALL THROUGH THE DAY

God is never the source of our anxiety.

MY DAY IS ENDING

With gratitude

Thank you for all the gifts of this day,
for being there for me
when doubt inevitably came

and threatened to replace
my confidence in you
with anxiety.
With your strength
I can send it on its way
like the temptation that it is.

With an offering

I offer you the silence of this night.
Let me offer it to you
peacefully,
without anxiety.
I offer all that I have done this day,
whether it was
defending myself against temptation
or welcoming joy.
It is, in your eyes, all the same.

And with a prayer for . . .

ONE FINAL WORD

This book was created to be nothing more than a gateway—a gateway to the spiritual wisdom of a specific teacher and a gateway opening on your own spiritual path.

You may decide that Francis de Sales is someone whose experience of God is one that you wish to follow more closely and deeply. In that case you should read more of him. His *Introduction to the Devout Life* on which much of this book has been based is the most available. You might also try his *Treatise on the Love of God*. But in many ways, the most readable and accessible of all his works are his letters. There are many editions, each offering a different selection.

You may, on the other hand, decide that his experience and teaching has not helped you. There are many other teachers. Somewhere there is the right teacher for your own, very special, absolutely unique journey of the spirit. You *will* find your teacher, you *will* discover your path.

We would not be searching, as St. Augustine reminds us, if we had not already found.

One more thing should be said.

Spirituality is not meant to be self-absorption, a cocoon-like relationship between God and you. In the long run, if it is to have meaning, if it is to grow and not wither, it must be a wellspring of compassionate living. It must reach out to others as God has reached out to us.

True spirituality breaks down the walls of our souls and lets in not just heaven, but the whole world.